The Consul General's Shanghai Postal Agency 1867-1907

by Peter L. Koffsky

SMITHSONIAN INSTITUTION PRESS · CITY OF WASHINGTON · 1972

The Consul General's Shanghai Postal Agency 1867-1907

Peter L. Koffsky

SMITHSONIAN INSTITUTION PRESS

City of Washington

1972

SERIAL PUBLICATIONS OF THE SMITHSONIAN INSTITUTION

The emphasis upon publications as a means of diffusing knowledge was expressed by the first Secretary of the Smithsonian Institution. In his formal plan for the Institution, Joseph Henry articulated a program that included the following statement: "It is proposed to publish a series of reports, giving an account of the new discoveries in science, and of the changes made from year to year in all branches of knowledge." This keynote of basic research has been adhered to over the years in the issuance of thousands of titles in serial publications under the Smithsonian imprint, commencing with *Smithsonian Contributions to Knowledge* in 1848 and continuing with the following active series:

Smithsonian Annals of Flight
Smithsonian Contributions to Anthropology
Smithsonian Contributions to Astrophysics
Smithsonian Contributions to Botany
Smithsonian Contributions to the Earth Sciences
Smithsonian Contributions to Paleobiology
Smithsonian Contributions to Zoology
Smithsonian Studies in History and Technology

In these series, the Institution publishes original articles and monographs dealing with the research and collections of its several museums and offices and of professional colleagues at other institutions of learning. These papers report newly acquired facts, synoptic interpretations of data, or original theory in specialized fields. These publications are distributed by mailing lists to libraries, laboratories, and other interested institutions and specialists throughout the world. Individual copies may be obtained from the Smithsonian Institution Press as long as stocks are available.

S. DILLON RIPLEY
Secretary
Smithsonian Institution

COVER ILLUSTRATION: The United States Consulate General in Shanghai, 1880. Transmitted from Consul General David H. Bailey to Third Assistant Secretary of State Charles Payson, 31 March. Courtesy of the National Archives.

For sale by the Superintendent of Documents, U.S. Government Printing Office
Washington, D.C. 20402 - Price 60 cents
Stock Number 4700-0144

Foreword

This paper is the result of eight weeks' research, largely in the materials at the National Archives, with the purpose of reconstructing the historical development of the United States postal service in China, 1867–1907. Most of the data was found in the diplomatic and consular records of the Department of State, and consisted of largely isolated pieces of data, making generalizations difficult. Further investigation of this service is highly desirable, should additional materials become available.

This work was done as part of the Smithsonian Institution Undergraduate Research Assistantship Program during the summer of 1966, under the direct supervision of Mr. Carl H. Scheele, Associate Curator in Charge of the Division of Philately and Postal History. His suggestions and encouragement are gratefully acknowledged. Thanks are also owing to Mr. Arthur Hecht and Mr. Ralph Huss of the National Archives, for their inestimable help in locating the references needed.

Contents

Introduction

The Westerners who came to live in the Chinese treaty ports during the nineteenth century found in operation postal services which were ancient and extensive, but totally unsuited to their needs. A system for carrying government correspondence had been instituted during the Chou dynasty (1122–255 B.C.). Known as *I Chan* or "post-stages," these offices ultimately served vast areas by foot and horse couriers. By the time of Marco Polo's visit in the fourteenth century, there were 10,000 stations utilizing 200,000 horses. The Ch'ing dynasty (A.D. 1662–1911) maintained 15,000 stations for foot couriers carrying routine correspondence, and an additional 1600 stations, provided with horses or boats, for the transmission of urgent memorials, important officials, and so forth. The entire system was supervised by the Board of War at Peking, but the actual arrangements and responsibility were in the hands of the local officials at each station. The costs of the service were deducted on the local level from the taxes reported to the provincial Treasury, a method which, according to the Working Report for 1904, "is said to lead to many abuses." The Ch'ing went their traditional way, and the Westerners searched for a more acceptable means of communication.

Postal services open for public use originated much later than the government posts, probably during the fifteenth century A.D. As they finally developed, these *min-hsin chü,* or "people's letter offices," were managed by banks or merchant establishments which had set up postal routes in order to transmit their own business correspondence. The rates were always quite moderate and the management eager to provide special services where desired. These "letter-hongs," however, could offer only a few routes to foreign countries; and the total lack of official control, while permitting the offices to give efficient and reliable service, also prevented the establishment of a truly national network of lines on both profitable and unprofitable routes. Similarly weak in this respect were the local posts in many of the treaty ports, which sometimes formed mutual agreements or branches for inter-city deliveries. The *min-hsin chü* were strongly entrenched and proved a difficult force to overcome when the national postal service was finally established.

Still another Chinese mail system was that managed by the Imperial Maritime Customs, developing after 1858. By the Treaty of Tientsin of that year, the Chinese government agreed to carry foreign legation mails to and from Peking. The introduction of new, more efficient methods gained this customs service the support of Viceroy Li Hung Chang and the opportunity

1

to increase its coverage of the port cities by slow, experimental stages. The idea of a national postal system under the Customs service was first officially supported by Inspector General Sir Robert Hart in 1876, during the negotiations with Britain for the Chefoo Convention on Sino-foreign relations. As the body of this paper will show, however, it was not until 1896 that the promise of a centralized national system was realized.

Under these circumstances, many foreign countries chose to set up their own postal systems in China, usually based in Shanghai with branches in the cities where consulates were maintained. The British system was the first established, developing after Hong Kong was acquired as a central base in 1839. In the case of the United States, true involvement in China may be dated from 1844, when the Treaty of Amity, Peace, and Commerce signed at Wanghia granted to it a "most-favored-nation" clause—a guarantee that America would receive the same privileges as were granted to any other country. American trade soon became centered in the International Settlement at Shanghai. For many years, however, United States citizens in China could communicate with their homeland only through the various foreign mail services via Europe or through the irregular channel of private sailing vessels crossing the Pacific Ocean. Events in the United States, however, were leading toward the establishment of a regular mail steamship line to the West Coast. During 1848–1849, at the time of the California gold rush, regular New York-to-San Francisco service was established by the Pacific Mail Steamship Company. The transcontinental telegraph was completed, and the Central Pacific Railroad incorporated in 1861. With communications to the west obviously greatly improved, President Lincoln authorized a mail steamship service to China on 17 February 1865. The Pacific Mail Steamship Company received a contract to provide this service the following year; in 1867 the first mail delivery to Shanghai was effected, and the operation of the Shanghai Postal Agency began. It remained under the direction of the consul general in Shanghai until 1907, at which time an independent postmaster was appointed. The Shanghai office was only abolished as a result of the Washington Conference of 1921–1922, under which many special rights in China were renounced. During its years of operation, however, the Shanghai Postal Agency did much to secure communications between China and the United States.

American Postal Services in China, 1867–1896

The Development of Routes

On 2 May 1866 Shanghai Consul General George F. Seward wrote to S. Ledyard Phelps, the Agent in China for both the newly authorized mail steamship line between San Francisco and China and for the United States Post Office Department, regarding the most efficient manner of organizing the new postal service.[1] He advocated that preliminary distribution of the mails from the United States be made through the ports of Hong Kong and Shanghai, the latter to be served either by a branch line of the Pacific Mail Steamship Company, or by a closed-mail agreement with the British semi-monthly and the French monthly steamers out of Hong Kong. All mails for the southern ports (Foochow, Amoy, Swatow, Canton, and the British, Dutch, Spanish, French, and Portuguese possessions in the East Indies) would be sent via Hong Kong, while Shanghai would handle those for the northern ports (Peking,

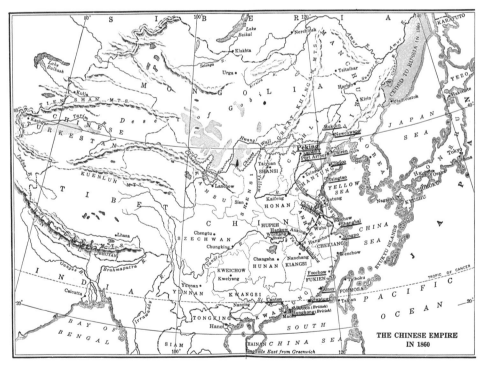

FIGURE 1.—Map of the Far East showing important cities. Adapted from Steiger, Beyer, and Benitez, *A History of the Orient* (Boston: Ginn and Company, 1926).

Newchwang, Tientsin, Chefoo, Hankow, Kiukiang, Chinkiang, and Ningpo). In each of these cities, the United States consul was to act as postal agent, in return for a "reasonable allowance" to be determined later and for the right to pay for necessary expenses out of postal receipts. A copy of Seward's memorandum was transmitted to the Secretary of State under the same date.

When the American postal system in China was formed in 1867, its procedures were basically those suggested by Consul General Seward, with certain modifications. Mails for the southern ports were indeed sent through Hong Kong, but a postal convention signed with the British colonial government there and ratified by the United States on 12 November 1867 provided that all mail be turned over directly to the colonial post office, for transmission to the British branch offices in the treaty ports.[2] Thus, no United States Postal Agent for Hong Kong was needed,[3] although the consuls at the various Chinese ports did continue to serve in the dispatching of official mails to Shanghai,[4] where correspondence to the State Department was supposed to be read and noted for informational purposes.[5]

In the North, however, the United States was obliged to make its own arrangements for the forwarding of mails to the various treaty ports. The first American mails reached Shanghai on 20 May 1867 after transfer outside the Yangtze estuary to a British steamer, and the first U.S. delivery direct to the harbor occurred on 3 August.[6] The Pacific Mail branch line between Yokohama and Shanghai, touching at Hiogo and Nagasaki, thus began operations to meet the trans-Pacific boats in Japan. It was the duty of the consul general at Shanghai to receive this mail and to arrange for its carriage to the addressee. In general the United States never maintained its own official mail routes within China, beyond the use of special couriers between Tientsin and Peking, and of messengers to deliver the mails in certain of the treaty ports once they had arrived—rather, the most efficient Chinese or foreign service available was utilized.

Although the Shanghai Postal Agency was the only full-scale dispatching and receiving center maintained by the United States in China, several consulates in the North also maintained an office to conveniently process the American mails.

As early as April 1868 the consul at Hankow wrote to the Shanghai agency regarding postal matters.[7] Each of the subsidiary agencies seems to have been provided by Shanghai with a supply of United States postage stamps, which were then sold upon application to those who wished to send letters from their port.[8]

This same system, with extensions, was continued throughout the period under consideration here. By 1889, when a list first appeared in the *United States Official Postal Guide,* mail could be sent from the United States via Shanghai to 20 Chinese cities (Chefoo, Chinkiang, Chungking, Hangchow, Hankow, Ichang, Kaiping, Kalgan, Kiukiang, Nanking, Newchwang, Ningpo,

Ourga, Peking, Shanghai, Taku, Tientsin, Wenchow, Wuchang, and Wuhu),[9] all served through the nearest United States consulate. For a brief period in 1882, the U.S. Post Office at San Francisco, lacking knowledge of Chinese geography dispatched the mails for northern China via Hong Kong. The vice consul general in charge at Shanghai made the following observation:

> Hong-Kong is nearly 900 miles south of Shanghai, and about seven days' passage from Yokohama, the same distances to this port. Letters directed to Tientsin, the most northern treaty port of China, and to Hankow, over 600 miles from Shanghai, on the Yangtse River, have not reached their destination until two weeks after the mail has been delivered at this port.[10]

This statement was enough to gain immediate instructions to San Francisco ordering resumption of the former routing system.[11]

The growth of the Japanese postal service changed U.S.-Chinese postal arrangements. On 1 January 1875, as a result of the postal convention of 6 August 1873 between the United States and Japan,[12] the United States postal agencies in Japan were limited to the exchange of mail beween Hong Kong and Yokohama,[13] and the Foreign Department of the Japanese Post was established. In March 1875 the Japanese Mitsubishi Mail Steamship Company purchased the Pacific Mail's Yokohama-Shanghai branch; and on 15 April 1876 a Japanese post office was opened at Shanghai, with branches at eight other ports (Chefoo, Chinkiang, Newchwang, Kiukiang, Tientsin, Hankow, Ningpo, and Foochow).[14] The subsidiary Japanese agencies closed for lack of business in 1881,[15] leaving communication with these ports to the British Hong Kong postal system.[16] The Japanese Shanghai office, however, quickly became a very popular means for dispatching mails overseas, as it offered a fast trans-Pacific route via Yokohama and thence by exchange on the American packets. The United States also arranged to have its mails carried on the same ships. The slowness of the American mail assembly procedure, however, caused by the fact that postal affairs had to take second place to regular consular business, kept the public use of its mails at a minimum. At the beginning of his administration in 1880, Consul General Owen N. Denny wrote, "all the labor of distributing the incoming mails fell to this office, while all of the revenue for outgoing mails went to the Japanese office."[17] Japan kept pressing for complete control of the transpacific mails as far as Yokohama, asking that the United States Agency at Shanghai be delivered over to their control. The United States, however, felt that the Chinese should be given the same chance for an independent postal system as the removal of American agencies in Japan had given the Japanese. It was decided, therefore, that we would wait for the formation of a native post system among the treaty ports, then under consideration, before giving up the Shanghai office.[18] The most immediate result of the Japanese demands was a general reorganization by Denny of the methods used at Shanghai, which resulted in a vast increase in American overseas mails leaving Shanghai,[19] creating new problems for every one of the consuls involved in the system.

Beyond Shanghai itself, the most important office in the American postal arrangement was that at Tientsin, the seat of the Chinese northern commissioner for foreign affairs.[20] As the gateway to the capital, the Tientsin office served as the United States' "only distributing postal centre for the north of China,"[21] in charge of all the mails to the legation in Peking. During the warm months from the beginning of March through the middle of December, the American mails arrived in Tientsin via coastal steamer from Shanghai.[22] The locally addressed matter was then delivered by a messenger employed by the consulate, "as is done at other consulates," while the mails for Peking were forwarded via special courier.[23] In 1887, following the improvement in Shanghai's service, consular official Smithers at Tientsin called attention to the new demands made upon his office, noting that "two and sometimes three large mail bags are received on the arrival of each U.S. Mail," and that "besides these mails there is an English mail for our citizens received from the English Postal Agency every week for delivery by this office."[24] Smithers requested that his office be provided with stamps on the same basis as the Shanghai office (i.e., as was a third-class post office, upon the filing of a bond to the Post Office Department),[25] and that an allowance of $250 (probably per annum) be given his agency "as compensation for distributing and forwarding the mails, attending to the sale of stamps, and for expenses for carrying the mails from the steamers to the office."[26] This request, however, was not accepted by Consul General Kennedy at Shanghai,[27] and nothing more seems to have been written on the matter. Finally, it should be noted that the Tientsin Consul also managed all mails to Shanghai[28] from his area. The Tientsin office seems never to have attained the rank of a full postal agency, and its cancellations as such an agency remain a mystery.[29] It was, however, an extremely important part of the American postal apparatus in China.

During the months that Tientsin was open to communication by water, the Peking legation received its mail regularly by a courier from that city. Difficulties, however, sometimes arose over the messenger service. From 1875 through 1880, the legation maintained its own official courier over this land route.[30] Following this period, a messenger dispatched by the American missionaries in Tientsin carrying their own mail to Peking was utilized, although the legation disliked this policy since "as their messenger is at most an ordinary Chinese servant, traveling on his master's errand, there is no sufficient guarantee of the security of our dispatches."[31] In 1885, Tientsin was ordered by Peking to send all legation matter via the Customs mail.[32] For the quarter concluded at the end of June 1894 this extra transportation of the mails cost the Tientsin consulate $27.83 in gold, which is described as "about the average amount paid quarterly for such service."[33]

During the winter period, when Tientsin was blocked by ice, it was necessary to carry the mails for Peking overland from Chinkiang, once they had arrived at Shanghai, "a twelve days' journey for a mounted courier through very unsafe country." [34] By the Treaty of Tientsin of 1858, the Tsungli Yamen (Chinese office for general management of matters concerning the various countries, a crude foreign office) [35] was responsible for the protection of these mails, and it very early arranged for the entire system to be managed by the Head Office of the Imperial Maritime Customs.[36] Starting on Tuesday, 13 December 1887, three dispatches of mail a week were sent from Shanghai to Chefoo, Tientsin, and Newchwang, as well as Peking, by the local customs authorities.[37] United States legation official Charles Denby noted in 1887 that the trip from Chinkiang to Peking took about thirteen days, covering 800 miles, the mail having first traveled by water from Shanghai, a distance of 157 miles.[38] Despite the distances covered successfully under very difficult conditions, Denby terms the service "irregular, slow and insufficient," since "it takes nearly as long a time to bring mail matter from Shanghai as it does to transport it to Shanghai from Washington." [39] Often delayed by the weather, the mail could take over twenty days to arrive at Peking.[40] This was a strong advertisement of the need for and potential direction of a more centrally organized national postal service, favored among the Americans by both Denby and the Secretary of State.[41]

Another American consulate which received a good deal of mail, having for a time its own handstamp, was that at Ningpo, just south of Shanghai.[42] In 1886, Edwin Stevens, former consul at Ningpo, noted that the Americans living at that port were "widely scattered, some being five miles apart, and that a consul is the custodian of the United States mails and is expected to deliver them free of charge." Stevens had for four years maintained a mail messenger at his own expense, and he now asked the Department of State to reimburse him for the $180 so spent, at four dollars per month, pointing out that the English consul received the use of a messenger plus $25 a quarter for his work in this respect. The department agreed to seek the amount either from current funds or through a special appropriation from Congress.[43] Early in 1887, the current consul, Thomas F. Pettus, wrote that he employed "a boy at eight dollars per month to receive and deliver mail daily to Shanghai steamers, also to receive and deliver the United States Mail on its arrival. He also delivers the mail when opened to the American and European citizenry at their homes"; the department was requested to aid in the payment of his wages.[44] Although the Customs post office maintained a service between Ningpo and Shanghai and, probably, thence via the Japanese office to the United States, it could not be used for consular mails because all official mail had to pass through the U.S. consulate general at Shanghai.[45] Ningpo ceased to have a separate consulate on 30 June 1896. As the postal services of the diplomatic officials were phased out, the mail was sent to a "reliable American," the Reverend J. R. Goddard, treasurer of the Baptist Mission at Ningpo.[46]

Still another major U.S. office was located at Hankow. In 1894, Consul Jacob Child requested "for a man to board the steamer and receive the mail, which is brought up the river by the kindness of the Captains of the boats, and after bringing it to the Consulate for distribution, deliver it to the various parties resident of the three cities Hankow, Wuchang, and Hanyang, seven dollars per month which is absolutely essential." He noted that from 100 to 300 pounds of mail were received at or dispatched from his office twice weekly, including many packages and much registered material and items with short-paid postage, and that it served a large part of the Yangtse Valley, at very little cost to the government.[47] This office seems never to have applied its own postal markings, as did Ningpo and Tientsin.

Thus, by 1896, the United States had built up a far-reaching group of consular post offices, connected to Shanghai by many different postal communication routes, for the carrying of official and public American mails. The American desire for a Chinese national postal service was evident, however, as seen in the legation's encouragement of the customs system and in letters quoted here. It was therefore a matter of high approbation for most of the American diplomats in China (with at least one notable exception) when, on 20 March 1896 an Imperial decree created the Imperial Post and named Sir Robert Hart to serve as the Inspector General of Customs and Posts.[48]

Administrative Difficulties

During this period the overall performance of the United States postal system in China was something less than satisfactory. Annoying delays between San Francisco and Shanghai, and a continual lack of sufficient manpower and funds at the latter port made it impossible to expedite the dispatch and distribution of the mails. The U.S. consuls frequently compared American efforts with those of other nations in a very unfavorable light, and requests from Shanghai to Washington that a special postmaster without consular duties be appointed were very common indeed.

The most frequent complaints received in Shanghai were from resident merchants who strongly disliked the slowness of the trans-Pacific steamers. Consul General Seward noted in 1870 that although the Pacific Mail Steamship Company authorities had not been "acquainted with Eastern ways of doing business," and had sometimes run "counter to the ideas of the resident merchants," and although the mails had frequently been late and irregular during the first 1½ years of service, the deliveries had for the past year been perfectly on time. Seward's only complaints were that the Yokohama agency had not been set up in an efficient manner, and that the foreign mail rates charged for letters sent through the American system were too high in the case of matter that traveled only between China and Japan or between ports within one of those countries.[49] By 1881, however, irregularity in the arrival of the

Pacific mails had once again become a problem for the merchants in China, much in contrast to the "prompt dispatch and receipt of the mails from Europe by the French and English Mail Steamers." [50] In answer to the complaints of Consul General Denny, the United States Post Office Department explained that the delays arose between the East Coast and San Francisco, not during the Pacific passage; for example, the New York mails had missed the sailing of one steamer that left in the middle of March, due to "snowstorms in the mountains." [51] In 1882, the Ningpo consul complained that the mails from San Francisco were apparently just missing the Japanese steamers leaving from Yokohama, thus having to be held for the next trip. The Secretary of State suggested that an agreement be reached with Japan whereby special bags containing the correspondence destined for Shanghai could be transferred in Yokohama harbor if the two ships passed each other there.[52] After an investigation, the Postmaster General replied that the trans-Pacific steamers had been causing the delays by failing to leave on the dates scheduled; problems also arose because the trip might take anywhere from 18 to 24 days. Far from leaving when they pleased, without any attempt to connect with the American mails, the Japanese steamers had often delayed their weekly sailing dates as long as 48 hours from the scheduled Wednesday departures. "As you can see," wrote the Postmaster General, "the special bag would do no good." [53]

In an attempt to improve the service, the postal authorities arranged in 1886 for mail to be carried on every trip of the Pacific Mail Steamship Company's boats.[54] This seems to have had little effect, however, for the next year Consul General Kennedy wrote of the Japanese steamers, that "as this line adheres to its own time-table, close connections with the Pacific lines are only 'happenings.' Not infrequently, an American Mail will be delayed in Yokohama a week and, in the meantime, another mail may arrive and thus we receive a double mail at Shanghai—which is annoying to merchants." [55] The question came up still again in 1896, at which time the Postmaster General promised only to request the Japanese office to take "such remedial measures . . . as may be practicable." [56]

The various consuls general also complained of their treatment by the State and Post Office Departments. The tone was set by Owen N. Denny in 1881, when he wrote that "there is saddled upon [this office] a lame [?] postal agency, which seems to receive comparatively little sympathy or support from any direction," and he asked that a salaried postmaster be appointed.[57] The year before, Consul General David H. Bailey had refused to file a bond for $10,000 with the U.S. Post Office Department, noting that he was already under bond to the State Department for that amount. Bailey also noted that the salary of the postal agent was only $25 per month, "every cent of which is paid to the clerk for performing the postal duties," which would make such a large bond an undue hardship upon the consul general.[58] He favored turning the agency over to the Japanese. Informed that he could not receive any postage stamps until he had filed the required bond, Bailey stated that he had twice explained his refusal to make the bond on the grounds that the business done by the agency, as well as the salary attached to it, was much too small. He now noted that during the first three quarters of 1878, under Guilford Wiley Wells, the agency had shown an excess of expenditure over income of $72.08 on receipts of $589.62, while in his five quarters of administration there had been an increase in the income and a decrease in the expenditures, leaving a net profit of $645.12 on receipts of $1667.23. Even with this increase, and despite the fact that the income from postal box rents went to the U.S. government, not to the postal agent, the Post Office Department had refused to increase the $300 per year salary. Bailey suggested to his successor Owen N. Denny that he might well feel the same dissatisfaction as he, in which case it would be necessary either to close down the agency or to place it in the charge of someone who would be willing to put up with the conditions involved in work "for which many postmasters in the United States receive from $1500 to $2400 per annum. I may be excused if I venture to observe that I do not think it possible to find such a person in Shanghai." [59]

Denny became Consul General at Shanghai in 1880 and filed his bond on 12 July [60] assured by the Post Office Department that as soon as the volume of business was large enough, he would be granted permission to employ a clerk for $100 per month, paid out of the revenue from the sale of postage stamps. The bond demanded was now only $5000. The consul general improved the service of the agency, and was able to increase "the revenue from about . . . $235 . . . per quarter to about . . . $735"; however, he was denied the help of a clerk, a situation which brought him to refuse extra work pressed upon him in 1881, relating to the making up of the mails for New York. [61] The additional work would, he stated, interfere with the work of the consulate general itself. The arrival of the mail necessitated the closing of the office for the remainder of the day, since the entire staff was needed to distribute it to Shanghai and to the outports. He was "quite at a loss to understand why the Post Office Department persists in dealing so parsimoniously with this Agency, when its liberality with its funds in other directions amounts in some instances, almost to prodigality." He complained once more about the delays caused to the mails in Yokohama. Denny regarded Japan as too unimportant a country in China to take full charge of U.S. mails, but he favored giving them over to the Chinese on their own territory as soon as possible. [62] Denny finally did receive authorization to spend $1200 per annum for a postal clerk, the full amount of which was given to the clerk. The latter could keep all of it, hire help with it, or otherwise expend the money so as to enable himself to "expedite the opening and delivery of the mails . . . ." [63] None of the other consulates seems to have been given special office help for postal affairs.

In 1885, the temporary head of the consulate general noted in a report that he was writing his dispatch at 11:30 p.m., while the deputy consul general and the marshal were engaged in making up the mails to San Francisco, which were to leave early the next morning, expending as they did so lighting gas that would have to be paid for out of the writer's own pocket, since there was no appropriation for it.[64] In the following year another temporary head complained that postage stamps, from which the expenses of the agency were paid, had not been sent, and recommended that a postmaster be appointed who would have sole responsibility for postal matters, for which he would receive "an adequate salary." [65] Consul General Thomas R. Jernigan agreed with this attitude when, in 1897, he asked to be relieved of the responsibility for the agency, only slightly mitigated by the presence of the vice consul general, then acting as postal clerk.[66]

This was also a period replete with scandals and accusations within the consulate general itself. The first occurred in 1877, when the vice consul general in charge, Mr. Oliver Bradford, was charged with having made fictitious vouchers among the expenses to be paid by the Post Office Department, having kept his postal agency books so as to gain an advantage from the exchange between silver and gold, and having opened and copied a letter passing through the agency from the surgeon of the consular jail to General W. Myers of the United States Army, in San Francisco.[67] Bradford was tried and convicted on the latter charge. Testimony revealed that the former Consul General John C. Myers had mistrusted Bradford when, as vice consul general, the latter had been responsible for the postal agency. Myers, however, had been suspended by Minister Seward before he could act against Bradford. It was also learned that Bradford had lived alone in the consular building, and that a number of letters had been received by the addressees marked "opened by mistake, O. B. B." [68] The ultimate disposition of this remarkable case is not made clear in the consular records.

A second accusation arose in 1880, when a Mr. L. B. Ring of Neillsville, Wisconsin, charged that mail sent between himself and Minister George F. Seward had been tampered with at Shanghai. Consul General Denny, beginning his improvement of the postal service, replied that "the complainant has been a little reckless in his statement," and that complaints made by Ring against Consuls General Myers and Wells, who had served during the 1870s, should have been made at that time. He further noted that the people currently working in the office, all appointed since Denny took office, were "so prompt and efficient . . . that the 'North China Daily News' paid them a handsome compliment in its issue of this morning for the prompt and careful distribution of the United States mails." [69]

Lastly, although it includes a small part of the period of the Imperial Chinese Post, there was the case of Consul General Jernigan versus his successor, John Goodnow. When he left office in 1897, after a term of three years, Jernigan found, according to his own dispatch in the matter, that there was due to his account as postal agent the sum of $259. This sum would be paid by the Post Office Department once the accounts had been passed, a question of three or four months. The compradore of the consulate general, who was charged with keeping the various accounts and with handling the office's money, refused Jernigan's offer to pay the amount from his own pocket and then wait for the reimbursing check, stating that, as he knew that the account was correct, he would send it in and allow the check from the post office to reimburse his own funds. Consul General Goodnow agreed to have the check from the post office made out in his own name, with provision that he would endorse it to the compradore. When the check was delayed because of a new administration in the Post Office Department, however, Goodnow cast aspersions against Jernigan's character, implying to the compradore that the money would have to come from the former consul general's bondsmen.[70] Thus, the administrative difficulties of this period ended with as little accord as that with which it had begun.

In conclusion, it should be noted that this period was one of growing general unrest and conflict in China. Riots against the ubiquitous Westerners began as early as 1868 in Yangchow and 1870 in Tientsin.[71] These disturbances clearly presaged the Boxer uprising of the turn of the century, which will be discussed in its postal context in the following section. More immediately disruptive was the Sino-Japanese War, which was declared on 1 August 1894 and which finally officially ended by a peace treaty signed on 17 April 1895.[72] On 4 October 1894 Consul General Jernigan wrote to Assistant Secretary of State Edwin F. Uhl regarding Japanese spies in China, stating that owing to the uncertainty of the mails in China and Japan, "I have thought proper to send you a copy of my dispatch No. 28."[73] This "uncertainty," however, was to prove only a taste of the disruption of communications that war in China would bring.

The Chinese Imperial Post Office, 1896–1907

The Adjustment of Routes

On 20 March 1896 an Imperial decree established the Chinese Imperial Post Office, under the administrative control of Sir Robert Hart and the Imperial Maritime Customs Service. The United States had long sought the formation of such a service. As early as 1877, U.S. Minister George F. Seward had reported happily that it was the intention of the inspector general of customs, the same Sir Robert, to set up a postal system among the various open ports and the capital.[74] When the official decree for a national system finally came, however, Consul John Fowler at Ningpo was one of the first to comment unfavorably. It was later written of Fowler that "he would be absolutely miserable if he did not have a row with some one or serious grievance against some person or department of the Chinese administration." [75] Fowler believed that the new system would only hurt American interests in China, for it would bring the trade of that country more than ever under the control of the British. He pointed out that Americans were not dealt with fairly in the choosing of staff for the Customs service.[76] It was "to all intents the most powerful Agency for the development of English commerce in China. The whole system is pregnated with English ideas and aims, the personnel is almost entirely British. It has offices in London; its contracts for supplies are always sent to London." He favored keeping the then current system, whereby most of the mail service in China beyond the foreign systems was controlled by the Chinese themselves.[77] An entirely different viewpoint was that of Consul General Jernigan, who wrote that

whatever tends to make China more civilized will certainly be promotive of American interest, for China will then be better prepared to recognize our superior civilization, and will doubtless be more inclined than ever to turn to us; and to be admitted as a member of the Postal Union China will thus be placed in touch with the civilized world by an Agency that will reach every corner of her vast empire.[78]

The development of the services of the new Chinese postal system was extremely gradual, due to a lack of funds and to the necessity of gaining the support of the other native mail carriers.[79] On 1 July 1896 the existing Customs postal service was expanded to include additional offices.[80] Matter originating in China and addressed to a foreign country was turned over to the appropriate foreign legation (i.e., American, British, French, German, or Japanese) in Shanghai, or to the British in Hong Kong.[81] The Chinese office applied foreign

FIGURE 2.—Consul John Fowler, master-critic of the Chinese Imperial Post Office.
Courtesy of the National Archives.

postage stamps at Union rates in return for the same amount in Chinese stamps affixed by the sender.[82] There was a great deal of confusion regarding the collection of domestic postal charges in addition to foreign ones on Union mails, the exact nature of which is unclear from the consular records.[83] Part of the problem was the decision by China to charge extra postage for carriage over the costly winter route to the north.[84] In the case of letters addressed to the American legation, Chinese postage stamps were added to the covers at Tientsin, and the extra charges involved were collected in Peking at the end of each month.[85]

The complexity of these administrative conventions clearly indicated that full Chinese participation in the Universal Postal Union would be highly advantageous for the rapid development of communications facilities. An announcement from the Chinese office to the U.S. Shanghai agency, dated 24 June 1896, stated that a letter had been sent to the Union indicating an intention to join.[86] Under instructions dated 29 October 1896 Denby invited the Tsungli Yamen to participate in the Universal Postal Congress to be held in Washington in May 1897 in order to acquaint the Chinese with membership requirements.[87] The Chinese accepted the invitation on 14 January 1897;[88] and on 22 March they named one American and two British citizens, all in the employ of the Customs, as their representatives.[89] At the Washington conference, China found herself not yet ready to become a full member, although she did undertake to follow Union practices as fully as possible.[90] Recognizing the superior service offered by the foreign agencies for letters addressed abroad, she desired that these offices remain in operation even after China had become a full member of the Union.[91] Later, Chinese representatives signed the convention that resulted from the Sixth Congress of the Universal Postal Union, completed on 26 May 1906.[92] On 1 October 1907, however, the day that the provisions of the agreement were to go into effect,[93] China declared that she did not intend to join the Union.[94] Thus it was not until 1914, that she became a member.

Despite the confusion that attended the foundation of the Imperial Post Office, the intra-China American mails were quickly turned over to its care, in keeping with United States policy of allowing each country to handle its own postal affairs as far as it was able. On 12 February 1897, after the Imperial Post Office had announced new regulations with regard to mails carried between Chinese ports by a foreign postal system, Charles Denby wrote from Peking that the changes would not affect American mail, since the United States had no Union post office that maintained interport business.[95] Twelve days later, Consul General Jernigan wrote that "by the rules of the Imperial Chinese post-office the postage on our local mails to the outports, to the various Consulates and to the Legation at Peking will have to be paid, which will materially increase our postage account."[96] On 9 May 1899 L. S. Wilcox, the consul at Hankow, noted that the postal agency at his post had been discontinued, as he put it, some two years before.[97] By 22 March 1898 matters had progressed so far that a Consular Bureau memorandum to Second Assistant Secretary of State Alvey A. Adee questioned the advisibility of maintaining even the U.S. postal agency in Shanghai, stating that "while formerly all American mail for other ports was made up at Shanghai by our postal agent, at present this is all done by the imperial post and the Consul General keeps only a local post office." [98] Consul General Goodnow's lengthy report to Washington, dated 31 May 1898, recommended the continuance of the Shanghai postal agency on the basis of seven points.

Since the Imperial Post Office did not carry international mail, the Shanghai office was "a convenience to parties sending mail to America." The U.S. mails were sent in sealed bags directly to San Francisco, while mail sent through the Japanese post office had to be re-sorted in Japan, frequently missing the departure of the same boat and suffering delays of a week to ten days. As evidence of this convenience, Goodnow noted that in spite of the delays caused by the (Spanish-American) war, and in spite of the fact that the U.S. 5-cent goal postal charge was equal to $11\frac{1}{4}$ cent Mexican, while the Japanese charged 10 Sen, or 10 cents Mexican, he was selling many more stamps in each quarter of 1898 than he had in the same quarter of 1897 (see Appendix 3).

Second, it was "a convenience to parties receiving mail from America." Since the beginning of the current quarter, he had rented six new boxes to business firms who had formerly received their mail by the local post. Since 1 May 1898 eighteen families and firms had decided to make use of the general delivery window rather than let the customs handle their mail. Goodnow stated that the local service frequently took two days after posting to deliver a letter; four times in the last month he had received heavily water-damaged mail. Wrong deliveries were commonplace. Even the customs maintained a box rather than receive its mail through its own service.

Third, there was "much complaint as to the charges etc. of the local post." Goodnow related the case of a Reverend J. R. Hykes who had had to send a package to another city. The parcel was returned to him by the Imperial Post Office because he had paid the 10 cents per pound examination fee in stamps rather than in cash. Unable to reach the post office in time to catch the mail once more, he gave the package to a friend who was traveling to the destination city; thereupon, he was threatened with a fine of 50 taels by the post office. The consul general stated that "the Imperial Post has antagonized and is antagonizing patronage and until they are really organized to do business properly, I can not recommend that our mail interests be further put in their hands."

Fourth, Goodnow felt that it would be a terrible waste not to use the post office facilities as set up in the consular building, held by lease until 1900.

Fifth, "prompt and polite service" was, under the present system, provided to Americans by Americans.

Sixth, China was in no position to take over the trans-Pacific mails. All mail would have to go via the delay-prone Japanese mail, or via the Canadian Pacific English mails, which ran only once every 20 days.

Finally, Goodnow pointed out that no other country had discontinued its postal agencies. On the contrary, the Japanese and Russians were establishing new ones. Trans-Pacific communication with Shanghai was absolutely essential to American trade, since almost all the business of the Yangtse Valley and of northern China was done through that port.[99] Thus, even when shorn of almost all its functions within China itself, the Shanghai Postal Agency is seen to have played a very important role in postal affairs. The Postmaster General agreed that the Shanghai agency should remain "for an indefinite period."[100]

Despite this decision, the United States entered into negotiations with China designed to make her even more the master of her own postal affairs. On 31 March 1899, Minister Edwin H. Conger at Peking notified Secretary of State John Hay that, after several conferences between American and Chinese representatives, the Postal Secretary of the Imperial Chinese Postal Administration, Mr. J. A. van Aalst, on behalf of Sir Robert Hart, wanted to invite the United States to conclude a postal agreement.[101] Article 17 of the Universal Postal Convention of Washington, signed on 15 June 1897, at the conference which China had attended, made it "possible for a non-Union office to send its mail matter to all parts of the world franked with its own postage stamps provided a Union Office guarantees and pays whatever may be payable by way of transit fees." This was equivalent to becoming an actual member. China was about to conclude an agreement with the British in Hong Kong whereby her mails would be carried in the Union system, but she also wanted an efficient method of communication to the east from "the great emporium" of Shanghai. To this end, closed and open mails were to be exchanged between the United States and China. China also offered to distribute free of charge all mails, including parcels, "received from the United States Postal Administration or its Shanghai Agency," in return for the same service on its mails to the United States. The Shanghai Postal Agency was also to accept open mails destined for foreign countries via the United States, and China was to accept matter arriving from abroad via the United States, under the same conditions as she did mail originating here. Closed mails would go from China to "San Francisco, New York, and the principal United States cities . . . and even . . . countries beyond America." China, of course, would pay all transit charges for her mails, and Union regulations would prevail.[102] Truly, this seemed a means of solving all of the postal problems between China and the United States.

The American Postmaster General provided an amended text for the agreement designating San Francisco and Tacoma, rather than Shanghai, as the exchange offices, since the Shanghai agency was not a Union office.[103] This text was accepted by the Chinese, with hopes of a future adjustment of certain points, and signed on 1 February 1900. Haste in putting the agreement into operation was suggested by Minister Conger, since the French were also about to sign an agreement with China. The Imperial Post Office agreed to begin whenever the United States was ready.[104] Only four months later, however, the Boxers took Peking, and all plans for completing the arrangements were suspended.[105]

Following the conclusion of the Boxer disorders the Imperial Post Office proferred requests for a new convention through the American Minister in Peking.[106] By 1908, however, the United States was still without an agreement with the Chinese service. The Boxer Rebellion had thus further delayed the full participation by China in the postal affairs of the world.

In the interim the Imperial Post Office expanded and improved its services to a greater part of China. Through internal reorganization, the Chinese postal service attained a higher level of efficiency. Its administrative staff was gradually separated from that of the customs,[107] and in 1905 the system realized its first year on a self-supporting basis.[108] Rates were drastically reduced.[109] The delivery of mail had been expedited to such a degree that in 1904, Minister Conger noted

In connection with this [Boxer indemnities] it is interesting to note that over four hundred distinct payments have been made for which signed vouchers had to be returned, in some cases from remote parts of the country. The letters have all been sent through the Chinese Imperial Post Office and not one of them has ever been lost in transmission or even seriously delayed. [110]

Despite this progress, for one reason or another many American diplomats favored a return to a system of American postal offices in at least their own cities of assignment. One example involved the requests from the consulate at Chefoo. In 1903 Consul Fowler was urging the Department of State to establish an agency at his port. In May of that year, Consul Miller of New-chwang wrote to support Fowler's request.[111] Miller's letter sets forth clearly the need, as he saw it, for this addition to the American system. Mail sent from the United States via Japan could be distributed from Chefoo to Peking, Tient-sin, Newchwang, Port Arthur, and Dalny via the Chinese, Japanese, or Russian posts, saving the delays met under the then current system of serving those cities.[112] In 1907, Fowler again explained the need for a postal agency, thus endorsing a petition from certain Americans in the city. One of the primary concerns expressed in the petition was for a return to the recently discontinued Japanese practice of sending the mails for Chefoo in ships directly from Japan, a service long used by the American navy and recommended by Fowler in 1903. The consul reported that the Japanese had agreed to re-establish the route. The petition also called for an American post office in Chefoo, and here the consul thoroughly agreed. There were 6000 American citizens living in the area, for whom large mails were received; these became even greater when the fleet was in port. Yet, the Americans had to depend upon other postal offices, especially the much-distrusted Japanese, and they had no American parcel post or money order service.[113]

Fowler's request was refused by the State Department, which stated that in a similar case at Amoy the year before the Postmaster General had replied that

in view of the repeatedly expressed desire of the Government of China for the discontinuance of the foreign post offices now operating in China, and of the Post Office Department's expressed willingness to withdraw the United States Postal Agency at Shanghai when the other foreign post offices in China are withdrawn, it is not considered advisable to open other United States Post Offices in China at this time.[114]

The Postmaster General also cited a letter of 30 April 1902 from Minister Edwin H. Conger at Peking, which had outlined U.S. policy regarding Chinese postal development. Conger had stated that the foreign offices interfered with the postal service and sovereignty of China, and that they should be maintained only at Shanghai, where the mail routes abroad centered, and where China herself desired them to remain until her own facilities were ready.[115]

Another request was received in 1906 from the southern port of Amoy, which was served by the Chinese government via ships trading between the Philippine Islands and Hong Kong. Since the United States had no post office in Amoy, its mails could not be forwarded in a special pouch. Thus they were subject to delays in Hong Kong and to the Chinese rate of foreign postage. Often, letters for Manila were placed privately on "coolie ships" leaving Amoy, with the object of having the crew post them at a Philippine port and so avoid the exorbitant costs and delays. Once again, registry and money order service, under Shanghai, was desired.[116]

Finally, a request was received in 1908 from J. C. McNally, the consul at Nanking, 185 miles up the Yangtse River from Shanghai. The Americans there resented having to pay 5-cent postage through the Chinese, German, and Japanese post offices, while two trains a day connected them with Shanghai, where the cost was 2 cents. Postal money orders and registered articles had to be sent to the United States through Cologne, under a German-American agreement, despite the fact that both services were available in Shanghai.[117]

Notwithstanding the United States' advertised desire to give as much control as possible to the Chinese posts, in 1905 the U.S. Post Office Department changed the carrying of its mails to Peking, and, probably at the same time, to Tientsin, from the Chinese to the French service. Mails for Peking were supposed to be sent through Yokohama via the Japanese Post, addressed to the French post office; the latter office had declared itself prepared to deliver mails to residences throughout the Legation Quarter.[118] The Peking legation appealed the orders, noting that the French, unlike the Chinese, had no means of distributing the mails within the city, and were turning the mails over to the Chinese post office once they arrived in Peking. Early the following year, Peking telegraphed that all the Americans here and Tientsin formally complained to me very great delay delivery home mails which are still handled by the French. They request forwarding them directly from Yokohama by the Japanese, and in China by the Chinese. I concur; very desirable.

The Postmaster General replied that the United States mails for Chefoo, Peking, and Tientsin had been sent via Japan since the preceding April, and thus "the delay complained of is not understood at this Department." The mails were addressed to the French post offices at the three cities. The department further stated that it did not seem that the delivery could be improved by changing either of these routing decisions, and that the legation should send some of the delayed covers to Washington, where the department would do its best to take remedial measures.[119] Minister Rockhill noted sometime later that most of his mail was still received via Shanghai. The French were having the Chinese carry the mails to the French post office at Peking, where anyone living outside the Legation Quarter had to pick up his mail. He also mentioned that the mails sent by the Japanese via Dalny were transferred to the Chinese at New-chwang and then distributed in Peking through the same unsatisfactory French system.[120]

At the same time, the postal arrangements with the French at Tientsin were equally unsatisfactory. The French distributions were frequently three to five hours later than the delivery of the Chinese mails that had arrived in the city on the same boat; moreover, the French, with post offices in Tientsin and Peking only, could not get the mail to the 13 American missionary outposts in the area. Instead, the material was held at the French post office. It was then left to the missions to arrange final delivery through the Imperial Post Office upon payment of 2 cents per half ounce. Within the city itself, the Chinese delivery system was much better than that of the French not only because it was faster, but also because the staff could speak English. Furthermore French ships were forbidden by Chinese law to carry any non-Chinese mail other than their own (a system begun by Sir Robert Hart, under which the ships of a given nation carried mail from its own and the Chinese systems only, in return for a rebate on "special permits" to load and unload cargo outside of regular hours).[121] Therefore the French were disregarding the regulations by carrying the American mails. The English boats plying between Shanghai and Tientsin carried only the Chinese mails. Under these circumstances, Albert W. Pontius, in charge at Tientsin, strongly recommended that the American agency in Shanghai also make use once again of the Imperial Post Office.[122] State Department official Charles Denby concurred with Pontius and called for an end to the "multiplicity of branch offices of various nationalities" in China. Since the legation had already made its dissatisfaction known, with the State Department receiving no reply to its letter to the Post Office Department on the subject, Alvey Adee ordered that the Washington office be addressed once more.[123] No action was implemented in response to these appeals and the eventual resolution of this highly complex matter remains uncertain.

Another routing matter, which was satisfactorily resolved, was the effort at the Foochow consulate to have its mails managed directly at Shanghai instead of via Hong Kong, as had been done from the beginning of the American service. In 1897, W. C. Hixson, the United States marshal in charge at Foochow, forwarded a letter to this effect from the city's General Chamber of Commerce to the Postmaster General and urged that this change in routing be approved. It was estimated that from ten to fifteen days would be saved by eliminating the route south to Hong Kong. With steamers leaving Shanghai for Foochow every two or three days,[124] the Imperial Post Office agreed to carry the mail from Shanghai free of charge.[125] With the endorsement of Consul General Jernigan the change was made, and apparently it worked well in preventing undue delay. Furthermore, in February 1903 Consul Gracey successfully protested the projected placement of his office under the administrative control of the new Canton consul general, for that would have required the mails from Foochow to be taken south to Canton, via Hong Kong, just so that the consul general could read the dispatches. The ultimate time to Shanghai would have been fourteen to sixteen days, rather than the current thirty-six to forty-eight hours.[126]

Finally, one should note the matter of the distrusted Japanese postal system in Manchuria and North China. In 1904, the Post Office Department ordered that all mails made up in New York for Manchuria be sent in the posts to Russia.[127] The order was then modified, at the urging of Minister Conger,[128] to include the mails for Newchwang (one of the early treaty ports) in those sent via Shanghai.[129] By 1908, following the Russo-Japanese War, however, American mail for Manchuria was being sent by the trans-Pacific steamers and given to the Japanese Post at Kobe. In that year, Consul General William Straight of Mukden complained that his mails were not safe in the hands of the Japanese, and requested that they be sent in the diplomatic pouch to Peking, or to the consulate general in Shanghai, for transmission in the Imperial Post. The latter possibility was accepted.[130]

This attitude of distrust was also reflected from within the State Department when, in 1908, it directed Rockhill in Peking to utilize the Chinese post rather than send and receive his official mails directly through Yokohama. Although, time could have been saved through use of the Japanese post, via various lines to U.S. Pacific ports such as San Francisco, Vancouver, Seattle, Tacoma, and Portland, suspicion that the pouches would be compromised prevented the use of these facilities.[131] Even in 1908, the United States distrusted the intentions of Japan in the North.

Proliferation of Disputes

During the period from 1896 to 1907, a number of difficulties disturbed those in charge of the Shanghai Postal Agency. The delays caused by the Spanish-American War have already been mentioned (see p. 16), as have the various complaints against the Chinese Imperial Post Office relating to charges for domestic carriage of Union mails. As these last were being argued, there occured the greatest disruption of postal facilities of this period of American mails to China. On 13 June 1900 the Boxers occupied the city of Peking, cutting off all contact between the American legation and its government.[132] On 23 June Consul General Goodnow at Shanghai was ordered to "hold pouch until safe forward Peking or send it Consul Chefoo." Goodnow decided to wait until the ministers were heard from again.[133] All postal services were disrupted by the war that broke out through much of northern China.

Due to this disruption and with a need for carrying mail to and from the American troops involved in the ensuing military operations, the Postmaster General on 2 August 1900 created a Military Postal Service in China,[134] with a "Military Postal Station No. 1" to be established on 25 August. The station was to offer facilities for money orders, registry, the sale of postal supplies, and the handling of mails.[135] Thus, this station, set up to serve American military personnel, was the first American office in China that offered all practical domestic services, including money orders. In 1901, it also became the first to accept mail from the United States at domestic rates.[136] Postal service was eventually established at Peking, Tientsin, and Tongku.[137]

During these difficult months, civilian correspondence was carried on in a variety of ways. Governments with interests in China maintained their own couriers to carry instructions and intelligence. As the Chinese government was not able to carry on a regular mail service for much of the time, "the (American) Navy often carried (its) mails."[138] Peking was finally relieved by a joint foreign relief force on 14 August 1900, but all difficulties were not immediately resolved. On 17 December Vice Consul General John R. Hykes wrote from Shanghai that

this morning we received a mail from Peking and the latest dates were the 28th of November . . . The mails from the North are very uncertain and the over-land courier service which is our most rapid method of communication with Peking during the winter months is, in the present unsettled state of the country, subject to delays . . .[139]

It was not until 26 July 1901 that the Postmaster General ordered

the military postal service in China . . . be discontinued, to take effect September 1, 1901. Discontinue on the same date Military Station No. 1, China.[140]

A second order returned all American military mails in China to the "rates, classifications and conditions existing prior to the establishment of the exceptional service in that country."[141]

Following the Boxer troubles, postal matters in China seem largely to have returned to their condition before the war. Consul Fowler continued his complaints against the Chinese service. On 9 January 1902 he asked that a post office be established at each consulate, so that all the mails from the United States could be forwarded from Shanghai in sealed sacks by the first ship, regardless of its flag. Under the current situation, he wrote, bags addressed to each of the ports and containing all but our first-class mail were received in Shanghai and there turned over unopened to the "customs" post, which then would use only certain ship lines to transport them, often causing a week's delay.[142] Fowler clearly wanted to crush the foreign-controlled customs service. In 1903, however, another step was taken toward better relations between the American and Chinese offices. The foreign postal agencies in Shanghai had long been a problem for the Chinese customs, since mail matter entered the country there without having been inspected for dutiable articles. On 15 June, therefore, the U.S. Postmaster General provided that all letters and packages that the postal agent felt might contain such articles would be inspected by specially authorized persons from the Chinese customs service. If material on which duty should be charged was found, the agent would arrange for the collection of the money and then remit it to the Chinese. The U.S. agency at Shanghai was reminded that it must retain custody of all mails in its care and allow none but the addressee or his agent to open a sealed package.[143]

Further difficulties arose over the order of the Postmaster General which, in 1903, made domestic postal rates, classifications, and conditions applicable to mails exchanged between the United States and possessions, and the Shanghai Postal Agency. The original order stated that articles franked at the lower rates would be accepted "for delivery in Shanghai . . . or in the cities in China served through the United States Postal Agency at Shanghai."[144] This last apparently applied only to certain categories of mail. As Minister Conger put it, many people misinterpreted the order to signify "that they could send letters at domestic rates to Peking, Tientsin, and every other Chinese post office."[145] In order to end this practice, the Postmaster General directed on 20 February 1904 that the following be, in effect, added to the 1903 statement:

EXCEPT that the Postal Union postage rates and conditions shall be applicable to LETTERS, POSTAL CARDS AND PRINTED MATTER destined for said cities other than Shanghai, viz: Letters, 5 cents a half ounce or fraction of half ounce; postal cards, single, 2 cents, double, 4 cents; printed matter of all kinds, including periodicals from publishers for regular subscribers, one cent for each two ounces or fraction of two ounces.[146]

The cities involved were the same twenty as listed in 1889 (see pages 4, 5), plus Foochow. Even this amended order, however, did not solve the problem of fees. Minister Conger noted toward the end of July that Americans were still receiving large numbers of letters addressed to other cities of China and franked at the 2-cent domestic rate. Any deficit between the postage paid and the 5-cent Union rate was doubled when the charges were collected by the Chinese post office; for example, for two consecutive days the Minister had had to pay $1.30 and $4.20, respectively, in postage due.[147] By 1908, after fourth-class mail beyond Shanghai had been cancelled,[148] a Rates Leaflet in use at Shanghai stated that all "articles for places other than Shanghai are subject to Postal Union postage rates and conditions." Even higher postage could be charged by the Chinese for heavy articles sent to or from places not served by steam.[149]

The years 1904 and 1905 saw still another war in the Far East, this one between Russia and Japan. Some delay and disruption occurred, of course, in mail services via Japan to the United States, and in the contested areas. Consul General John Goodnow, returning to Shanghai, wrote on 1 March 1904, that he had been "delayed a few days in Japan by the break of communications owing to the war." [150] In December he found it necessary to return to the State Department letters directed to the American consuls at Dalny (Dairen) and Vladivostock, stating that "we have used every means in our power to get them to their destination and, being unsuccessful, return them to you." [151] The difficulty in receiving dispatches was probably a familiar problem for the Dalny consulate. In 1898, the Russians, in control of the Liaotung Peninsula, had refused to accept Chinese Imperial Post Office stamps on matter addressed to Port Arthur, demanding that all mail be posted at their office in Shanghai for transmission through their own system. [152]

In 1905, another complaint was made against the postal agency at Shanghai by a correspondent who had experienced trouble with his mail. While the accusation was easily countered, the matter clearly shows the difficulties under which the Shanghai office was operating at this time. Mr. John Franklin Crowell of the Intercontinental Correspondence University, wrote to Washington that "owing to the notorious carelessness and supreme indifference of the Consular post office," it was necessary for all mail sent to him through the agency to be registered. Consul General James Linn Rodgers replied that great care was exercised in the handling of all mail, and that those persons who kept locked boxes or called for their mail at the general delivery window had no trouble at all with missing letters. If the items were intrusted to the Chinese Imperial Post delivery, with which the agency had a contract, however, some carelessness might be met. In the case of mail matter addressed to interior points, which was turned over to the Chinese for transmission with receipts taken for the bags alone, [153] even more difficulties were likely. Much of the material so transferred was stamped, even at this late date, at domestic postage rates, the collection of extra charges for which was a chore for the native post, especially since many items had to be returned to Shanghai because the postage due was refused by the addressee. Rodgers pointed out that the responsibility of the American system ended when the mail was turned over to the Chinese either for local or interior delivery; any attempt to trace a missing item through the Chinese post, he added, usually failed. [154]

The following year, the Chinese Imperial Post Office began to complain about the practice of franking letters addressed to a foreign country maintaining postal offices in China with the stamps of that country at the low overseas rate available only at the Treaty Port agencies, and then sending such covers to these ports in another envelope through the Chinese post office. One thus avoided the more expensive Union rates to foreign countries. The matter had first appeared in the consular files in 1904, when Consul L. S. Wilcox of Hankow wrote that a Reverend A. E. André of Fan Cheng (north of Hankow)

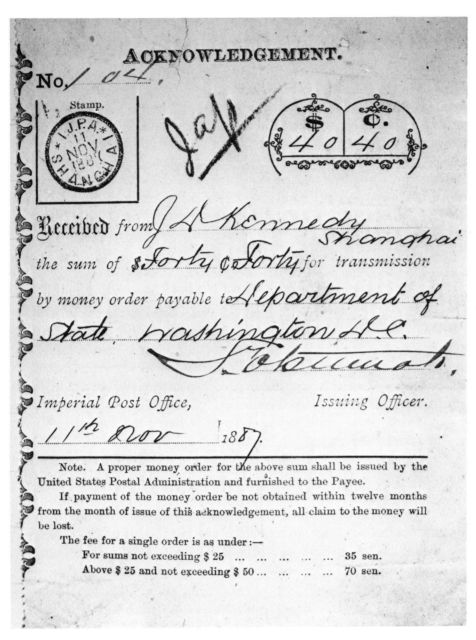

FIGURE 3.—A receipt issued by the Japanese post office in Shanghai, showing the use of foreign postal services in transmitting money from the United States Consulate General to the Department of State. Courtesy of the National Archives.

had complained to him that the local post office had suddenly halted the practice by refusing to accept such covering envelopes. Reverend André noted that all foreign mail matter except letters was retaxed upon delivery in Fan Cheng, even if franked at Union rates, and stated that at least the right of cheap communications with home enjoyed at Shanghai should be given to those Americans living in other cities.[155] On 19 November 1906 the Chinese Imperial Post Office in Foochow issued an official circular, noting that "numerous letters have recently been received at this Office" regarding the matter. The circular stated that such a practice could not be allowed, as it was "an evasion of the rights of the Chinese Imperial Post"; furthermore, it claimed, all other postal systems forbade circumventing postal charges by using covering envelopes. In his dispatch accompanying this circular as sent to the Department of State, Consul Samuel L. Gracey also included copies of two other letters on the subject. On 9 October 1906 the Deputy Postmaster of the Imperial Post Office at Shanghai had written to a Reverend W. N. Brewster in Foochow, stating that

I have as promised referred to Peking the question re. sending your International letters under cover to friends in Shanghai for posting as U.S.P.O. and B.P.O. and am able to inform you that it is satisfactory from a Postal point of view.

On 1 December Gracey wrote to John Gardner Coolidge, the chargé d'affaires in Peking, noting that the circular's quote from the British laws was not, as claimed, from the postal guide, but from a (unidentified) private letter, and that the International Postal Union and U.S. regulations seemed to contain no such provisions as the Chinese mentioned. The matter was suspended until further rulings could be obtained from Peking.[156] In this case the various parts of the Chinese postal administration seemed to have very little idea of what the others were doing.

Finally, as the period of Shanghai's administration by the consul general ended, a case arose which highlights the confusion resulting from all the different postal administrations operating in China. The Consul at Tsingtau, Wilbur T. Gracey, had complained to Washington that postal authorities in the United States had refused to accept parcels addressed to his post city. In reply, he was told that Tsingtau was located in the German leased area of Kiaochow, and that thus

articles for Tsingtau are included in mails subject to the stipulations of the United Postal Convention, which convention makes no provision for the transmisson, at less than the letter-rate fully prepaid, of packages of miscellaneous merchandise other than samples having no salable value.[157]

Packages of merchandise addressed to cities other than Shanghai had had to be delivered in China through foreign postal systems with a branch in the city involved since the use of the U.S. domestic fourth class rate applicable to some such places had been cancelled in 1906.[158] Apparently, no parcel post agreement had been signed with the German offices in China, although such conventions were operating with at least the offices of Japan and of Hong Kong.[159]

The year 1907 saw a very complex postal situation in China, replete with unsatisfactory service and great confusion. The Chinese Imperial Post Office was seeking to extend its services so that membership in the International Postal Union and improved domestic methods could make possible the removal of all competing lines and provide China with a single, rapid mail system. In Shanghai, the United States Postal Agency was placed under the administration of a full-time, salaried postal agent, with the hope that his myriad duties would now be more fully and successfully performed. It was not, however, until 1914 that China entered the Union;[160] foreign postal agencies remained until the end of 1922.[161]

Notes

National Archives

Seventeen files of material were utilized at the National Archives. They are listed below with the Record Group number under which each is included. See References for complete citations of published works. Shortened citations are given in the notes following.

General State Department Records (R.G. 59)

Instructions
Miscellaneous Letters
Numerical File

State Department Records by Post (R.G. 84)

Amoy
Canton
Chefoo
Foochow
Hankow
Newchwang
Ningpo
Shanghai (Consulate General)
Tientsin
Dispatches, Peking to Tientsin
Peking (Legation)

Post Office Department Records (R.G. 28)

Orders of the Postmaster-General
Post Office Department Journal
Press-Copy Letterbook of the Postmaster-General

Post Office Department Library

Miscellaneous Orders of the Postmaster General. Bound volumes.

1. National Archives, Shanghai, 2 May 1866.

2. U.S.P.O.D., *Annual Report 1867*, pp. 129–130.

3. *Ibid.*, p. 22.

4. Dispatch of 12 September 1868. In a register of materials received. National Archives, Shanghai, 13 October 1868.

5. For the difficulties in obtaining compliance from the Canton office, see National Archives, Shanghai, 12 March 1883. Other offices also caused difficulties.

6. Lobdell, "Beginnings," pp. 18 and 20.

7. In a register of materials received. National Archives, Shanghai, 11 July 1868. Unfortunately, the dispatches themselves cannot be found.

8. National Archives, Shanghai, 13 February 1882.

9. *United States Official Postal Guide*, series 2, vol. 11, no. 10, p. 23.

10. National Archives, Shanghai, 16 September 1882.

11. National Archives, Miscellaneous Letters, 30 October 1882.

12. U.S.P.O.D., *Annual Report 1873*, pp. 123–128.

13. National Archives, Instructions, 22 January 1875.

14. Lobdell, "Beginnings," pp. 35–36.

15. *Ibid.*, p. 36. See also *United States Official Postal Guide*, series 2, vol. 4, p. 784.

16. *United States Official Postal Guide*, series 2, vol. 4, p. 784.

17. National Archives, Shanghai, 13 February 1882.

18. National Archives, Peking, 16 April 1879.

19. National Archives, Shanghai, 13 February 1882.

20. Fairbank, *East Asia*, p. 317.

21. National Archives, Tientsin, 2 September 1887.

22. National Archives, Tientsin, 14 December 1894.

23. National Archives, Tientsin, 2 September 1887.

24. *Ibid.*

25. National Archives, Shanghai, 20 March 1880. The document dated 19 March is enclosed in this dispatch.

26. National Archives, Tientsin, 2 September 1887.

27. A note of 3 September 1887, written on the dispatch.

28. National Archives, Dispatches, Peking to Tientsin, 10 October 1887 (vol. 4, p. 153).

29. Cancellations reading "U.S. Postal Agency, Tientsin" are known for the late 1880s and early 1890s; they are identical in type to that of Shanghai, which also appears on the envelopes. For what little has been published on this matter, see Sloane, "U.S. Varieties," vol. 13, no. 1, and vol. 28, no. 10.

30. National Archives, Dispatches, Peking to Tientsin, 5 December 1881 (vol. 3, p. 51).

31. *Ibid.*

32. National Archives, Dispatches, Peking to Tientsin, 28 April 1885 (vol. 4, p. 90).

33. National Archives, Tientsin, 2 July 1894.

34. Chinese Directorate General of Posts, *Report, 1921*, p. 6.

35. Fairbank, *East Asia*, p. 316.

36. Chinese Directorate General of Posts, *Report, 1921*, p. 6.

37. National Archives, Peking, 14 December 1887.

38. *Ibid.*

39. National Archives, Peking, 14 February 1887.

40. *Ibid*, 14 December 1887.

41. *Ibid.*

42. An oval handstamp from the "United States Consulate, Ningpo, China" is known with dates in the early 1890s. The mail then passed through Shanghai on its way to the United States. See Sloane, "U.S. Varieties," vol. 13, no. 1, and vol. 28, no. 10.

43. National Archives, Ningpo, 15 March 1886.

44. *Ibid.*, 31 January 1887.

45. *Ibid.*, 19 January 1887.

46. National Archives, Shanghai, 30 July 1896.

47. National Archives, Hankow, 15 October 1894.

48. Chinese Directorate General of Posts, *Report, 1921*, p. 7.

49. National Archives, Shanghai, 20 April 1870.

50. *Ibid.*, 26 December 1881.

51. National Archives, Miscellaneous Letters, 20 May 1882.

52. *Ibid.*, 30 October 1882.

53. *Ibid.*, 23 January 1883.

54. National Archives, Instructions, 25 October 1886.

55. National Archives, Shanghai, 25 August 1887.

56. National Archives, Miscellaneous Letters, 30 October 1896.

57. National Archives, Shanghai, 14 November 1881 (Annual Report).

58. *Ibid.*, 3 February 1880.

59. *Ibid.*, 20 March 1880. The document dated 19 March is enclosed in this dispatch.

60. National Archives, Shanghai, 12 July 1880.

61. National Archives, Miscellaneous Letters, 5 December 1881.

62. National Archives, Shanghai, 13 February 1882.

63. *Ibid.*, 27 March 1897.

64. *Ibid.*, 24 September 1885.

65. *Ibid.*, 4 May 1886.

66. *Ibid.*, 3 April 1897.

67. *Ibid.*, 23 October 1877. Also 20 November 1877. The document dated 22 October is enclosed in the latter dispatch.

68. National Archives, Shanghai, 20 November 1877.

69. *Ibid.*, 14 May 1880.

70. *Ibid.*, 23 October 1899.

71. *Ibid.*, 27 August 1895. The document dated 20 August is enclosed in the dispatch.

72. Livingston, "R. A. de Villard," p. 58.

73. National Archives, Shanghai, 4 October 1894.

74. National Archives, Peking, 23 April and 17 December 1877.

75. Note attached to dispatch. National Archives, Chefoo, 23 January 1903.

76. The indoor staff of the Customs as of 25 January 1899 was British 175, Continental European 90, American 16, Russian 9. The United States maintained one-tenth to one-seventh of the trade, but received only one-eighteenth of the jobs. National Archives, Shanghai, 29 January 1899. The document dated 25 January is enclosed in the dispatch. This letter shows just how little the Chinese had to do with the management of their own customs service, or with that of the mail service it controlled.

77. National Archives, Ningpo, 10 June 1896.

78. National Archives, Shanghai, 4 March 1897.

79. Chinese Directorate General of Posts, *Report, 1921*, pp. 7–8.

80. National Archives, Peking, 2 May and 3 July 1896.

81. *Ibid.*, 3 July 1896.

82. Chinese Directorate General of Posts, *Report, 1921*, pp. 8–9.

83. National Archives, Shanghai, 2 July 1898. The document dated 15 June is enclosed in the dispatch. Also National Archives, Chefoo, 23 January 1903, with enclosures. Fowler claimed that the Chinese had broken an agreement of 1897 to transmit "fully prepaid" American mail matter in the open mails between Shanghai and "interior Chinese Post Offices," free of additional charge to the addressee. United States postage

stamps were to be used. It is doubtful, however, that the agreement pertained to Chefoo at all, or in all seasons, nor that the principal case, relating to carriage that probably occurred during the Boxer Rebellion, would have fallen under it anyway. It is also unclear whether or not parcels would have been included. For a highly colored account of the process by which the Imperial Post took over American mails, see the almost constant stream of dispatches directed by Fowler to the State Department, beginning on 24 February 1897, National Archives, Chefoo.

84. National Archives, Peking, 31 March 1899.
85. *Ibid.,* 31 December 1896.
86. *Ibid.,* 26 June 1896. The document dated 24 June is enclosed in this dispatch.
87. National Archives, Peking, 31 December 1896.
88. *Ibid.,* 15 January 1897.
89. *Ibid.,* 23 March 1897. The document dated 22 March is enclosed in this dispatch.
90. Chinese Directorate General of Posts, *Report, 1921,* p. 8.
91. National Archives, Miscellaneous Letters, 13 July 1898.
92. National Archives, Numerical File, 4375 (vol. 389), 3 June 1907.
93. Second Assistant Postmaster General, *Report, 1906,* p. 182.
94. National Archives, Numerical File, 4375/33 (vol. 389), 11 November 1907.
95. National Archives, Peking, 12 February 1897.
96. National Archives, Shanghai, 24 February 1897.
97. National Archives, Hankow, 9 May 1899.
98. National Archives, Shanghai, 14 February 1898.
99. *Ibid.,* 31 May 1898.
100. National Archives, Miscellaneous Letters, 13 July 1898.
101. National Archives, Peking, 31 March 1899.
102. *Ibid.,* 31 March 1899. The document dated 30 March is enclosed in this dispatch.
103. National Archives, Peking, 8 June 1906.
104. *Ibid.,* 1 February 1900.
105. *Ibid.,* 4 November 1903.
106. *Ibid.*
107. Butler, Report, 6 February 1908, National Archives, Numerical File, 8526/2–4 (vol. 614).
108. *Ibid.*
109. National Archives, Newchwang, 12 April 1902.
110. National Archives, Peking, 22 June 1904.
111. National Archives, Chefoo, 23 January 1903.
112. National Archives, Newchwang, 22 May 1903.
113. National Archives, Numerical File, 7705 (vol. 576), 21 June 1907.
114. National Archives, Numerical File, 7705 (vol. 576), 29 July 1907.
115. National Archives, Peking, 30 April 1902.
116. National Archives, Amoy, 11 June 1906. For the request of the new consul general at Canton for a postal agency at his post, see the dispatches dated 20 April and 24 July 1903, National Archives, Canton.
117. National Archives, Numerical File, 13827 (vol. 856), 21 April 1908.
118. National Archives, Miscellaneous Letters, 22 April 1905.
119. *Ibid.,* 22 January 1906.
120. National Archives, Peking, 30 March 1906.
121. Chinese Directorate General of Posts, *Report, 1921,* p. 8.
122. National Archives, Numerical File, 1481 (vol. 165), 29 August 1906.
123. National Archives, Numerical File, 1481 (vol. 165), 10 October and 13 October 1906, respectively.
124. National Archives, Shanghai, 3 April 1897.

125. National Archives, Foochow, 29 March 1897.

126. National Archives, Shanghai, 11 March 1903. The document dated 18 February is enclosed in this dispatch.

127. *United States Official Postal Guide,* series 2, vol. 26, no. 6, p. 9. This is General Order 576, dated 12 May 1904.

128. National Archives, Peking, 3 July 1904.

129. *United States Official Postal Guide,* series 2, vol. 26, no. 10, p. 13. This is General Order 588, dated 29 September 1904.

130. National Archives, Numerical File, 8526/10–11 (vol. 614), 15 April 1908.

131. *Ibid.,* 16360 (vol. 959), 22 September 1908 (and notes) and 21 September 1908.

132. National Archives, Shanghai, 25 June 1900.

133. *Ibid.,* 29 June 1900.

134. National Archives, Orders of the Postmaster-General, journal 5, p. 459. This is order number 911½, dated 2 August 1900.

135. *Ibid.,* p. 454. This is order number 912, dated 2 August 1900.

136. *Ibid.,* pp. 670–673. This is order number 395, dated 30 March 1901.

137. U.S.P.O.D., *Report of the Third Assistant Postmaster General, 1901,* p. 800.

138. National Archives, Chefoo, 23 January 1903.

139. National Archives, Shanghai, 17 December 1900.

140. National Archives, Orders of the Postmaster-General, journal 6, p. 141. This is order number 933, dated 26 July 1901.

141. *Ibid.,* p. 165. This is order number 1008, dated 23 August 1901.

142. United States, State Department, *Foreign Relations . . . , 1902,* pp. 222–225.

143. National Archives, Orders of the Postmaster-General, journal 7, pp. 223–224. This is order number 534, dated 15 June 1903.

144. *Ibid.,* p. 183. This is order number 441, dated 30 April 1903.

145. National Archives, Peking, 4 November 1903. There is evidence that the Postmaster General misjudged his power to change the rates for mail conveyed beyond Shanghai.

146. National Archives, Orders of the Postmaster-General, journal 7, p. 575. This is order number 147, dated 20 February 1904. Emphases are taken from the *United States Official Postal Guide,* series 2, vol. 26 no. 3, p. 6.

147. National Archives, Peking, 26 July 1904.

148. United States, Washington City Post Office, *Postal Information,* p. 1.

149. National Archives, Numerical File, 8526/2–4 (vol. 614), 6 February 1908. A sample of the leaflet was enclosed in this dispatch and is bound with it.

150. National Archives, Shanghai, 1 March 1904.

151. *Ibid.,* 1 December 1904.

152. *Ibid.,* 5 September 1898. The information is contained in an article from the *North China Daily News,* 3 September 1898, which is included in the archival material.

153. All mail matter for the interior was turned over to the Chinese for promised delivery at no charge above Union rates. See National Archives, Chefoo, 23 January 1903, for excerpt from Superintendent of Foreign Mails dispatch to Consul General Jernigan, 30 June 1897, Number 133311.

154. National Archives, Shanghai, 30 October 1905.

155. National Archives, Hankow, 23 July 1904. The André letter is dated 8 July 1904.

156. National Archives, Numerical File, 3841 (vol. 352), 9 October and 1 December 1906.

157. National Archives, Numerical File, 9185 (vol. 666), 4 December 1907.

158. United States, Washington City Post Office, *Postal Information,* p. 1.

159. For the agreement with Hong Kong, see National Archives, Orders of the Postmaster-General, journal 8, pp. 109–110. This is order number 830, dated 26 July 1904. For that with Japan, see National Archives, Orders of the Postmaster-General, journal 8, pp. 159–160. This is order number 958, dated 25 August 1904.

160. List appears in the *United States Official Postal Guide,* series 3, vol. 7, no. 1, p. 130.

161. United States, State Department, *Foreign Relations . . . , 1922,* pp. 291–292.

References

Chinese Directorate General of Posts, Supply Department. *Report on the Chinese Post Office, 1921.* Published 1922.

Fairbank, John K., Edwin O. Reischauer, Albert M. Craig. *East Asia: The Modern Transformation.* Boston: Houghton Mifflin Company, 1965.

Livingston, Lyons F. "R. A. de Villard and the Stamps of China." *The Collector's Club Philatelist,* vol. 28, no. 1 (January 1949).

Lobdell, H.E. "1867, The Beginnings of Scheduled Trans-Pacific Mail." *Twelfth American Philatelic Congress* (1946).

North-China Herald, 4 October 1907.

Polland, W. Scot. "Mail Service to China and Japan in the Nineteenth Century." *Western Express,* January 1965.

Sloane, "U.S. Varieties" *Stamps Magazine,* vol. 13, no. 1 (5 October 1935), p. 21, and vol. 28, no. 10 (9 September 1939), p. 337.

United States, House of Representatives. "Postal Accounts with Shanghai and Tientsin, China." House Document 704, 59th Congress, 1st Session.

United States, Senate, Select Committee on Methods of Business and Work in the Executive Departments. "The Cockrell Report, 1888." Senate Report 507, 50th Congress, 1st Session.

United States, State Department. *Foreign Relations of the United States.* 1902, 1922.

United States, Washington City Post Office. *Postal Information,* vol. 2, no. 14 (2 April 1906). Available at the Post Office Department Library, Washington, D.C.

United States Official Postal Guide. Series 2: vol. 4 (January 1882); vol. 11, no. 10 (October 1889); vol. 26, no. 3 (March 1904); vol. 26, no. 6 (June 1904); vol. 26, no. 10 (October 1904). Series 3: vol. 7, no. 1 (July 1914).

United States Post Office Department [U.S.P.O.D.]. *Annual Report of the Postmaster General,* 1867, 1873. [The titles of the published annual reports change frequently.]

——————. *Report of the Auditor for the Post Office Department, 1895.*

——————. *Report of the First Assistant Postmaster General, 1902.*

——————. *Report of the Second Assistant Postmaster General, 1906.*

——————. *Report of the Third Assistant Postmaster General, 1901.*

Appendix 1

Development of the Postal Services
at Shanghai

The Shanghai Postal Agency was founded by the Post Office Department on 10 June 1867, when the Postmaster General wrote to the Secretary of State by special messenger, requesting that he appoint the consul general at Shanghai "to receive, distribute, deliver, and dispatch the correspondence conveyed by United States Packets to and from [that] port." [1] On the same day, the State Department approved the appointment, directing that separate

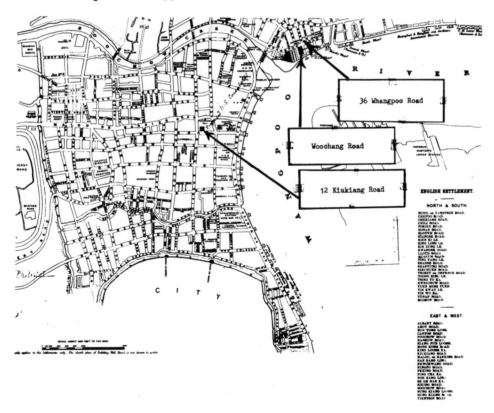

FIGURE 4.—Map of Shanghai showing locations of the various U.S. consulates general. Basic map courtesy of the National Archives.

accounts be kept for the two functions of the consulate general, as the Post Office had agreed to defray the postal expenses, and enclosing a certificate of appointment and a letter of instructions from the Postmaster General.[2] The actual Postmaster General's order was made on June 14;[3] and on 14 October, Vice Counsel General Mangum acknowledged the appointment on behalf of Consul General Seward.[4]

The service offered by the Shanghai agency slowly grew more extensive than that of simply receiving and dispatching letter and papers. Boxes were first made available for rental in 1870.[5] In 1887, Consul General Kennedy wrote that

It is very gratifying to know that, through representations made by me to the Post Office Department, samples of merchandise can now be sent to the United States as Fourth-class matter, and not at Letter rates, as had been previously exacted.[6]

Another such added service, long desired by the American businessmen in China, was that of the domestic money order. In 1899, Consul General Goodnow wrote to the State Department, enclosing an advertisement from the Japanese Post Office offering money orders to be sent to the United States, and strongly suggesting that this country take advantage of this impetus to trade by offering its own service.[7] An example of the receipt issued by the Japanese in acknowledgement for their orders, in this case used by Consul General Kennedy in 1887 to transmit a payment from the estate of a deceased American to his heirs in the United States,[8] is pictured here. Goodnow's request was refused, however, in a letter from the Postmaster General to the Secretary of State, dated 19 December 1899. Under the law, it was impossible to establish a domestic money order office in a foreign territory.[9] By 1902, however, the law had apparently changed, and on 22 March of that year, in answer to further requests from Shanghai, the consul general was authorized to issue money orders.[10]

On 19 August 1902 the Postmaster General issued an order that made the service to Shanghai even more useful for businessmen whereby the Postmaster at San Francisco was to make up supplementary mails for the China steamers, closing them not more than one hour before the steamer sailed. Letters carried in these mails were to be prepaid at "double the rates applicable to similar articles in international mails."[11] It was now possible to send last minute articles in each mail.

The greatest boon to American trade came, of course, when domestic postage rates were made applicable to "articles passing between this country and [the Shanghai] Agency." The superintendent of foreign mails notified the consul general on 9 May 1903, that the service would be conducted upon that basis beginning on 1 June; Goodnow replied on 9 June that it would indeed be "a great advantage to Americans in China and to American trade."[12] A side benefit to the consular service was that now, under domestic mail classifications, the official correspondence between Shanghai and Washington could be transmitted in penalty envelopes.[13]

The period 1867 to 1907 also saw a great growth in the popularity of the American system for mail transportation. Much of this has already been mentioned, in discussing the disputes between various consuls general and the Washington departments. By 1888, the Select Committee on Methods of Business and Work in the Executive Departments reported the Shanghai Postal Agency had four employees, who received salaries of $100, $15, $8, and $5 per month, respectively.[14] In 1905, Vice Consul General Davidson reported that the office handled "some four thousand bags of mail a year".[15] One year later the Consular Bureau stated that the agency handled about 12,000 bags per annum, receiving about 200 bags at a time. The American office exceeded the German in volume of mail handled but was slightly exceeded by the English.[16] Whether either or both of these figures are correct, a large volume of material was passing through the consulate general by 1907.

On 25 September 1907, after years of repeated urging on the part of many consuls general, the Shanghai Postal Agency was taken from under the responsibility of that officer. John M. Darrah had earlier in the year been appointed deputy marshal at the consulate general, in order to fill a gap between departing and arriving marshals.[17] He had also worked for some time within the postal agency itself.[18] In September, acting under authority which he had held since the 1860s [19] but chosen not to use, the Postmaster General ordered that

John M. Darrah is hereby appointed United States Postal Agent at Shanghai, in China, and his compensation is fixed at twenty-three hundred dollars ($2,300) per annum, United States gold.[20]

Now, for the first time, a full-time agent devoted his efforts to managing and improving the service at Shanghai.

Notes

(See pages 28–29 for full National Archives and U.S.P.O.D. Library references. See page 34 for complete citations of publications.)

1. National Archives, Miscellaneous Letters, 10 June 1867. Bound in the volume marked on the spine as pertaining to the first part of June 1868.
2. National Archives, Miscellaneous Letters, 10 June 1867. Bound in the volume marked on the spine as pertaining to the first part of June 1868. Unfortunately, the letter of instructions from the Post Office Department has been lost.
3. National Archives, Post Office Department Journal, vol. 63, p. 304, 14 June 1867.
4. National Archives, Shanghai, 14 October 1867.
5. National Archives, Post Office Department Journal, vol. 68, p. 621, 9 May 1871.
6. National Archives, Shanghai, 25 August 1887.
7. *Ibid.*, 19 February 1899.
8. *Ibid.*, 11 November 1887.
9. National Archives, Miscellaneous Letters, 19 December 1899.

38   SMITHSONIAN STUDIES IN HISTORY AND TECHNOLOGY

10. U.S.P.O.D., *Report of the First Assistant Postmaster General, 1902,* p. 166.
11. National Archives, Orders of the Postmaster-General, journal 6, p. 594. This is order number 929, dated 19 August 1902.
12. National Archives, Shanghai, 9 June 1903.
13. National Archives, Instructions, 23 December 1903.
14. United States Senate, Select Committee, *The Cockrell Report, 1888,* Part 3, p. 6.
15. National Archives, Shanghai, 27 March 1905.
16. *Ibid.,* 24 February 1906. Consular Bureau memorandum attached.
17. National Archives, Numerical File, 552 (vol. 80), 1 February 1907.
18. *North-China Herald,* 4 October 1907, p. 7. See also United States House of Representatives, "Postal Accounts."
19. U.S. Statutes at Large, Section 7, Act of 27 July 1868 (15 Stat. Chap. 246).
20. Post Office Department Library, Miscellaneous Orders of the Postmaster General, vol. 12, order 719, 25 September 1907.

Facilities and Equipment Available to the Postal Agency

The developing situation and services of the Shanghai Postal Agency may be seen clearly in the physical facilities and tools available to it at different times during this period. In 1868, for example, as the agency was first being established, the only likely indication in a consular inventory that such an office existed at all was the presence of "1 stamp 'Forwarded by U.S.C.'"[1] (The dating stamp of the Consulate General was definitely used as a postal marking, appearing as early as November 1867.[2] A Special "P.O.D." dater is reported in use the following year.[3]) Very little equipment was available.

In 1874, Consul General George F. Seward signed a lease agreement, at his own risk, for a consular compound to be built to his specifications, with a main entrance off Woochang Road, on the banks of the river, in the American concession. As seen in a floor plan drawn in 1885, the post office was here situated in virtually a single room on the ground floor of the main building, immediately to the left as one walked down the corridor.[4] By 1878, the office was well provided with various pieces of equipment, as will be seen from the inventory below. Entries where the writing is not sufficiently clear for positive identification, are noted with a question mark.[5]

2 large forms (boxes for firms)	1 memo. request book
1 large sorting table	5 old style mail bags
1 receiving [reading?] table	5 new style mail bags (canvass)
1 set alphabeticle [sic] boxes (letters)	3 letter boxes for steamers
1 set alphabeticle [sic] boxes (papers)	1 pkg. wrapping paper
3 upright distributing boxes	1 twine box & lot of cotton twine
2 small distributing stands	1 shelf for weighing letters [?]
1 stamping table	1 ink stand
1 set pigeon holes for Chinese letters	1 leather mail bag
1 table	3 ink pads
1 candlestick	4 cancelling stamps
3 post office scales	2 date stamps with type
1 spring balance scale	1 register stamp with type
1 copy book letters sent	1 missent & forwarded stamp
1 register of registered letters	1 due stamp
1 register of letter book [?]	1 paid stamp

1 paid in full stamp	1 U.S. Postal Guide
1 unpaid stamp	3 vols. Postal regulations
1 not found stamp	1 large iron safe
1 advertized stamp	1 too late stamp
1 unclaimed stamp	1 tax stamp
1 returned for postage stamp	Sundry forms
1 unsufficiently [sic] prepaid stamp	1 U.S. Post Office sign

This is the only full inventory of the post office contained in the Shanghai consular records.

In 1885, the owner of the land and buildings, David Reid of London, England, grew tired of having his rent set at low levels by the Congressional appropriations, and sold the property to the Japanese Mail Steamship Company.[6] In 1888, this company informed the Americans that it would be necessary for the consulate to be vacated on the following 1 February. Consul General Kennedy was forced to rent space in a row of tenements that were to be put up on a back street in the heart of the business district of the British concession, because the high rents charged in Shanghai put all other land far beyond the reach of the consulate.[7] The new buildings were delayed because of heavy rains,[8] but on 1 April 1890 the move was made to 12 Kiukiang Road. Consul General Joseph A. Leonard wrote that

in the back of the [second] story is the Post Office twenty eight by twenty feet in size with a room twenty by thirteen feet alongside for the use of the coolies. The Post Office is much better arranged and more convenient for the distribution of mails than it was in the building removed from.[9]

The building was so situated that this country's flag could not be seen from the harbor,[10] but the financial situation made it necessary in 1899 for the lease to be extended through to 31 March 1901.[11]

In late 1900 or early 1901, Consul General Goodnow agreed to rent the premises then occupied by the Club de Recrio, with a ten-year lease that would begin when certain repairs and changes, to be started on 1 June, were completed.[12] The site, at 36 Whangpoo Road, was in the American Settlement, only a block away from that of the buildings commissioned by Seward in 1874. The lease was signed on 1 August 1901 to begin on that date.[13] This position of the consulate general was still not completely to the liking of patriotic diplomats, since it was located on a street behind the warehouses of the Japanese Steamship Company;[14] it was, however, in the American portion of the city. The facilities for the post office originally constituted one room. In 1905, however, Consul General Rodgers wrote that

the Post Office has been allotted one back room, accessible to the public only by a species of alley known as Old China Street, which abuts on the Eastern side of the premises. As the mail for Shanghai, and for other places in China, coming into this office, has been increasing with every month, and as Americans of Shanghai have complained bitterly of our postal accommodations in comparison with those of other nations, it seemed but

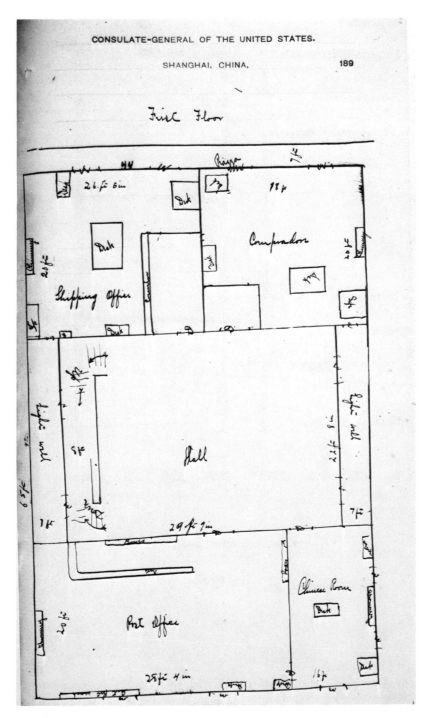

FIGURE 5.—Floor plan of the post office at 12 Kiukiang Road, 1897. Transmitted by Consul General Goodnow to Assistant Secretary Day, 12 November. Courtesy of the National Archives.

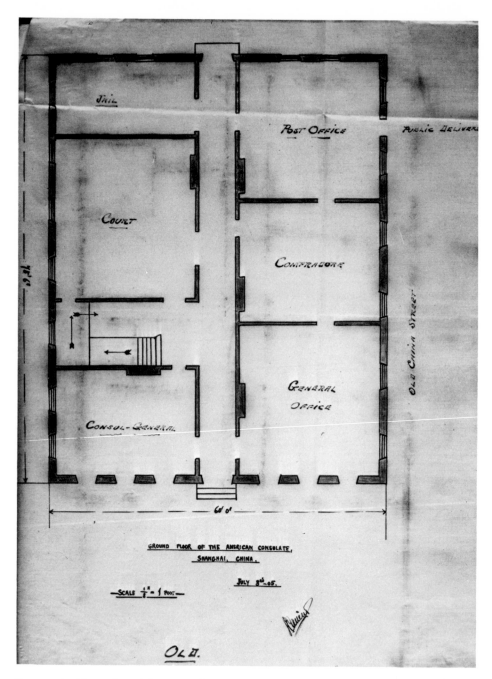

FIGURE 6.—Floor plan of the post office at 36 Whangpoo Road, 1905. Transmitted by Vice Consul General in charge Davidson to Assistant Secretary Loomis, 27 March. It appears that enclosures in the Shanghai file, Record Group 84, National Archives, were confused before the documents were bound. This figure appears to have been in Rodgers' letter to the Department of State, 6 July 1905. Courtesy of the National Archives.

justice to the department to give it the space it pays for, and at the same time to afford the public conveniences and facilities, which were impossible under the old arrangement.

The Post Office will have the East half of the first floor, which will permit of the installation of a requisite number of lock-boxes, money order and stamp department, besides providing a lobby into which the public can go for their mail and other postal business.[15]

These new accommodations included four rooms: Receiving and Dispatching Room (25 feet by 21 feet); Post Office, Registry, Money order, Stamps, General delivery, Mail boxes (25 feet by 27 feet); Assorting and Compradore Room (25 feet by 21 feet); Lobby for those calling for mail (8 feet by 25 feet). Despite this

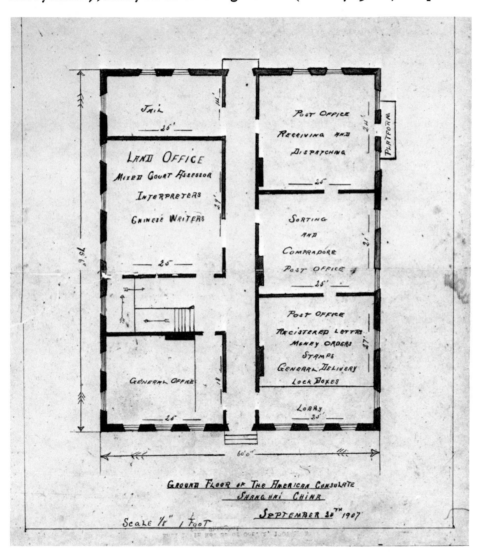

FIGURE 7.—Floor plan of the post office at 36 Whangpoo Road, 1907. Transmitted from Consul General Denby to the Assistant Secretary of State, 2 October. Courtesy of the National Archives.

enlarging of the office, Consul General Charles Denby, who replaced Rodgers in 1907, felt called upon to complain to the State Department that there was still not enough room for the office or for the lock boxes demanded, nor was there room for a private office for Mr. Darrah, who has just been appointed to his post. The surroundings were not at all conducive to the conduct of business.[16] This may well have been true, but the offices then occupied were the best ever held by the postal agency, and they seemed quite likely to be the best obtainable from Congress for many years to come.

Notes

(See pages 28–29 for full National Archives and U.S.P.O.D. Library references. See page 34 for complete citations of publications.)

1. National Archives, Shanghai, 7 April 1868.
2. Lobdell, "Beginnings," p. 25. The stamp, at the lower left of the envelope, is dated 27 November 1867.
3. Polland, "Mail Service," p. 15. An illustrated cover, sent from Peking on 27 October 1868, was handstamped in Shanghai on 20 November.
4. National Archives, Instructions, 23 December 1874. See also National Archives, Shanghai, 30 October 1885.
5. *Ibid.*, 26 September 1878.
6. *Ibid.*, 24 September 1885 and 3 February 1888.
7. *Ibid.*, 9 August 1888 and 26 June 1890.
8. *Ibid.*, 14 November 1889.
9. *Ibid.*, 26 June 1890.
10. *Ibid.*, 24 May 1895.
11. *Ibid.*, 6 October 1899.
12. *Ibid.*, 22 January 1901.
13. *Ibid.*, 27 November 1900 and 5 October 1901.
14. National Archives, Numerical File, 651/1 (vol. 96), 11 September 1906.
15. National Archives, Shanghai, 6 July 1905.
16. National Archives, Numerical File, 651/7–13 (vol. 96), 2 October 1907.

Appendix 3

Chinese Currency and Accounting

One of the most difficult problems faced by the Shanghai postal agent was that of accounting for the monies received and spent as part of his job. Until 1894, the official unit of currency in China was the tael, which, according to E. J. Smithers in Tientsin,

is a weight of pure silver, and is the highest that is applied to the precious metals. It is not a coin, but is nevertheless the common medium of exchange in all commercial transactions throughout the empire. It differs from the currency of Western nations inasmuch as it represents no fixed value, its value varying according to the scales in which it is weighed.[1]

The tael was then divided by weight into mace and candareen; each candareen then equaled ten copper cash.[2] Actual transactions were made in bank notes, silver bullion, copper cash, or foreign currency.[3] The value of the tael in relation to foreign currencies was often changed, with Treasury circulars advertising the changes taking weeks to arrive in China.[4]

In 1894, the Mexican dollar, in use since the eighteenth century, was adopted as the official Chinese currency, called the *yuan*. At that time, it was worth about 50 cents in American gold.[5] Although a coin, the Mexican dollar was also valued only for the silver it contained, its worth depending upon the silver market at any given time. Other coins in use, such as those representing dollar fractions, which were less fine and called "small money," and the copper cash, even varied in value in relation to the dollar.[6] Under these circumstances, it was extremely difficult to maintain any idea of the value to the Post Office Department of money received and spent at the Shanghai agency. The complex question of exchange rates and premiums figured highly in the 1877 charges against Vice Consul General Bradford,[7] and created many problems.

In 1899, in an effort to stabilize the situation in regard to the sale of postage stamps, Consul General Goodnow requested that he be authorized to sell 5-cent stamps for an even 10 cents Mexican, as did the other offices under the Universal Postal Union. Because of the exchange rate, he had been forced to sell the stamps for "practically 10½ cents Mexican."[8] Belatedly, the Postmaster General issued order number 287 of 1 March 1901, in which he stated that the agent was hereby authorized to receive Mexican silver at 50 per cent of its face value in exchange for United States stamped paper. When the Mexican silver thus received is exchanged for American currency the postal agent shall submit with his quarterly postal account a sworn statement of the transaction. An allowance will be made to cover any loss resulting from the difference between the commercial rate of exchange and the rate herein authorized, and the postal agent should claim credit therefor in his quarterly postal account.[9]

This system remained in effect until 1 July 1908, after which time Mexican money could be accepted only at the current rate of exchange, and only if the transaction entailed no loss to the United States government.[10]

Finally, there was the very real problem of maintaining a regular financial interchange between the Post Office Department and far-away China. In 1895, for example, it was suddenly discovered that no settlement of the Shanghai accounts had been made since 1879, and that no remittance of income had been submitted since 1884. The matter was remedied by an order of 1 April 1895, which made the agency accountable at the end of every quarter, as would be an ordinary postmaster.[11]

Notes

(See pages 28–29 for full National Archives and U.S.P.O.D. Library references. See page 34 for complete citations of publications.)

1. National Archives, Tientsin, 3 September 1887.
2. National Archives, Tientsin, 30 September 1875.
3. Livingston, "R. A. de Villard," p. 57.
4. See, for example, National Archives, Shanghai, 7 April 1887.
5. Livingston, "R. A. de Villard," p. 57.
6. Young, "The U.S. Postal Agency," pp. 339 and 341. See also list of rates for the Chinese Imperial Post Office in National Archives, Numerical File, 9526/2–4 (vol. 614), 6 February 1908.
7. National Archives, Shanghai, 20 November 1877 (with enclosures) and 2 May 1878.
8. National Archives, Shanghai, 19 February 1899.
9. National Archives, Orders of the Postmaster-General, journal 5, p. 642. This is order number 287, dated 1 March 1901. On 1 April 1905, however, the agent in Shanghai announced that "postage stamps and postal cards will be sold at the rate of exchange fixed by the American Government quarterly." He then ceased claiming an allowance for exchange. See United States, House of Representatives.
10. Post Office Department Library, Miscellaneous Orders of the Postmaster General, vol. 12, order 1387, 20 May 1908.
11. U.S.P.O.D., *Report of the Auditor for the Post Office Department, 1895*, pp. 641–642.

152